Another Saturday Night in Jukebox Hell

Poems by Alan Catlin

ROADSIDE PRESS

Another Saturday Night in Jukebox Hell
Copyright © Alan Catlin, 2024
ISBN: 979-8-9902309-1-0

Cover Art: Gene McCormick
Editor: Michele McDannold

Roadside Press
Colchester, Illinois

toc

"It's four a.m. and the sky is getting lighter, like a threat."

Eliza Clark

Terminal Cases

This is the bar where beer goes
to turn flat in lines that have not
been cleaned for thirty years,
lines so thick with slime and yeast and
bacterial waste only the scum filters
through with liquids unfit for human
intake though the men who drink
here neither notice nor care.
Their eyes no longer focus.
Their mouths no longer taste,
though nothing stops them lighting up
between sips, between gobs of blood
coughed up and spit on the floor
where more than one of them
will go to die. No one asks questions
about how it has come to this or why;
this is why they are living; it's just
what they do.

Lady Day Sings the Blues in the Open-All-Night-Club

When the Resurrection Jazz Band
takes the stage to play in Hell
there will be a dearth of instruments:

tall black flutes,
reeds stained by eternal fire,
rusty valves soldered to their frames,
impossible to move

Toy pianos and tiny kid drums
too undersized to play

Bent tin horn bored by plumber's snakes,
the router's tip still dangling from
a well-chewed spout beside
crude painting on the dented shaft

And the headless jazzmen will all be dressed
in their identical red suits,
furious fists clenched the burnt sienna air
amid a choking wedge of flame

Lady Day strokes the blues,
the reds, the white hearts,
out of the ever-loving night

high on death and tea bag dreams,
her voice a razor blade
and this open-all-night-club the skin

"many doors to hell; open, all of them open." (2)
David Peace

The one you choose is always
the wrong one, there can be no
other way. The sky so deliberately
absent here, a thicket of black snow
the bellhops clear a path through
with rusty blades, leaving streaks like
blood drops of oil light is filtered
through, stains in the hereafter, now.
The air is heavy, breathing is a chore
like building a fire without flames,
fording a river without shoes.
On the other side, the neon DON'T
WALK signs are flashing, sink holes
where sewer drains should be,
curbside hydrants flushing the streets
with acetylene up near the roof of
the cave where the ruined buildings
should be, helium balloons, each one
a gondola filled with ashes Buddhist
monks spread on the streets below,
doors open and shut everywhere around
you but you can no longer see.

"many doors to hell; open, all of them open." (3)
David Peace

all of them inviting you inside,
the air so cold it hits you in the chest
like a fist, a hammer alongside the head,
the room spinning like a "Strangers on
the Train" out of control merry-go-round,
all the overhead lights flashing, disorientation
complete until the guess-your-weight guy
hands you a card and points down to the pit
where the mud wrestlers are grappling in
the muck, the packed-in-tight crowd
placing bets, money clenched in their fists
as they cheer their champions on as if
the women were not human but fighting cocks
and this was a winner takes all contest to the death
and all the blood splattered on the walls was
not forensic evidence of some horrible crime
you have witnessed and participated in,
hand still clutching the card given at admittance,
the one that says GOOD FOR ONE FREE RIDE
IN THE TUNNEL OF LOVE, a voyage in the dark,
the ride of a lifetime, a ferryman waiting inside,
holding a lantern, beckoning for you to follow.

"alone and insane in tiny rooms"
Bukowski

This is the way the world looks
near the end, all the city's junk
collected and safely stored for
the mass combustion, accelerants
provided, in fifth floor walkup
now that the elevators no longer
work, all the stuff no one needs
bagged in corners, an open morgue
for daily racing form news,
late scratches, telephonic transmissions
she wrote down on salvaged scraps:
hot dog wrappers, deli sandwich
papers, air sickness bags, pooper
scooper packets, using blood from
a thousand paper cuts for ink, stuff
she photocopied and collated,
only the outline images of what she
wrote clear, all the words invisible,
"the way they should be" she
whispers to herselves in self-imposed
darkness, munching on dead insects
stored in wrinkled brown paper bags,
"the best ones are the hard-shelled ones,"
she says watching the snow fall in
between channels on portable no cable

TV, alone and insane in tiny rooms,
four feet of garbage between her and
a locked fire door, single window
hermetically sealed by grime, a perfect
kind of darkness inside, customized
for smoking her own special brand
of, acquired-from-the-street, loco weed.

The laughing heart

"Life is on the wire, everything else is just waiting."
    Karl Wallenda

When she still had a job
her nickname was Speed Queen,
an appellation earned from
dead end relationships with
a series of lean, no account,
bad teeth boyfriends who lived
in way outback trailers in some
woods off no name dirt roads
not mapped out yet and likely
never would be. Every time
her cell rang, she thought it was
that Mission Impossible guy
with an assignment so outrageous,
how could she refuse to take it?
After a week of higher than a Byrds
song from the 60s without sleep,
she thought the phone told her
where to go, what to do when she
got there, but not what to do after.
All of it so horrific, it might even have
been something like the truth but
once the deed was done and the dead
bodies rolled over and examined,

she conceded the voice might actually
have been one from *A Nightmare on
Elm Street* and that she was a bit confused
at the time the instructions were received.
None of which mattered once the verdict
had been read and the judge decreed she
would get one last needle for a magic,
stainless steel table carpet ride no one
ever came back from. Once all the appeals
had been exhausted, the governor's pardon
denied, not even a jailhouse conversion
could save her.

There Were Giants in Those Days

"The body of the boy lies on the asphalt
like the body of a boy." Ilya Kaminsky

Before the war, the poet says that
he and his wife had made a child.
Then the war took them both away.
The grief that followed was worse
than the chains they clothed him in,
the solitary rooms they locked him in.
Worse than the meals of dried bread
and dirty water he fought the rats for.

Released, he became a prophet
of the depraved. Wore what prisoners
wore: rags and scars. Found himself
on stages at anarchist conventions,
fronting neo-punk bands playing
four string, two chord guitars
and a-chased-by-furies, tone deaf,
dead beat drummer.

The song cycle lyrics he spouted grew
like mushrooms on his tongue.
Drew crowds to the stage like lemmings
to the cliff. Heeded their call to walk
like a star struck jesus, on hands extended

like plywood boards building a green mile
for him to stride all the way
to a burning cross.

Found Photo:
Alexandra like a Wraith from the Psych Ward

Long before she was cast in
the role of Our Lady of Lost Souls,
she had been instructed on the ways
of the oracle, of the order,
by inanimate objects, plaster statues
that spoke in tongues she had a personal
holy book for, new lines inscribed daily
by an invisible hand on paper that had
to be burned to reveal the secrets
they contained or held up to dressing
table mirrors so that the backward writing
could be made clear. Sleepless nights,
she prayed with the glass beads that
hung from all the fixtures, door handles,
bookshelves, each one assigned an hour
of the wolves to be worshipped with, not
one minute more nor one less. She was told
the way would not be an easy one,
only those pure of flesh, completely
mortified could proceed, continue
while others fled, leaving thorns,
straight pins, darning needles behind,
those objects, she would need to proceed
once the skin has been made to cohere,
made to feel the healing begin, like those

stigmata scars she shared with the spirits
who whispered in her ears after dark no matter
where she was confined, teasing her hair
after, in morning rooms she rehearsed
chapters and verses from the books after
Revelation, the ones so sacred they
must never be written down or spoken of
by anyone not among the anointed
the way she was.

Wasted

"You've always been alone
By now it is your trademark
You like it that way."
 Frankie Bono, "Blast of Silence"

Twenty-four years of hard drinking
and all I have to show for it is a bleeding ulcer,
a bank account with no balance, one way
canceled tickets to Hell and a conductor
telling me that if I didn't slow down
soon, I'd be lucky to live much past
forty. I'm not sure where the luck
figured in, if my life, the way it was,
is what living is all about: four walls
lined with dead soldiers, a leaky gas stove
spewing so many fumes no headache
cure could relieve, a radio that only received
transmissions from people whose lives
were over before they began, uneasy listening
hours, scherzos by Paganini's evil twin,
music so demented the walls bled vibrations,
shuddered in my sleep, my life so wasted
I wondered how I managed the energy to breathe.

The Introduction

After the initial exchange of names,
if she liked the way you looked,
she'd put her other hand, not shaking
yours, on your thigh, stare into
your eyes, move closer as she held
a look that suggested you could be
more intimate with her than anyone
else ever could, ever had been, might
move in closer still, briefly lick your
lips then step back and wait for your
next move; no matter what happened
next, it was going to be your fault.

"some babbled and some prayed"
Bukowski

as if end time was yesterday
and they needed more money
for the meter that had run out,
the red arrow pointed directly to
expired, indulgence money to insure
that next time the call was issued
and the righteous revived, they would
be among the numbered, the elected
to be lifted from their riding mowers in
mid-row or from the bridge table
completing a double slam bid,
iced cold Coors Light and blender made
Mojito on hand for the trip, Extreme Unction,
the rockabilly band playing the airwaves
as their personal tower of power,
lyrics fit for the ballpark or the ultimate
home invasion in their ears, hoping,
as it happened, for another turn,
another shot at the spinning prayer
wheel of life ever after. Maybe when
the winds from nowhere fanned fires
burned out, the blackened earth cooled,
the seas replenished, maybe, then, it would
be their time.

Living the Dream

After Power Point presentations
in hotel lounge playing the macho
fool for the ladies, wedding ring impression
clearly visible to all who care to look,
jejune banter endlessly fascinating to
the all night, pay-as-you-go girls,
for whom all pick up lines are as fresh
as yesterday's beside-the-road-kill.
A couple of intimate drinks in low light
lounge, she looks like a goddess in
high heels, ready to rock and roll with
room service libations and pay per view
porn, so willing and available no price
mentioned or discussed, he thinks he is
the luckiest of God's creatures scoring big
on good looks and charm, one night away
from heaven on a half-shell, though his reality
has a stomach pump in it, an overdose
administered while he is in the head,
room ransacked by professionals, anything
of value long gone, not even the lingering
scent of hundred dollar an ounce perfume
left behind.

The Dancing Girls of Death

She was fifteen going on,
a Sex in the City age, three gold
rings in her right ear, a clown's-
head charm bracelet around each
wrist, and a blue butterfly tattoo
on her butt, no one in her family
had seen nor, ever would, if she
had her way. "My stepdad would
freak if he knew. Especially, as he
paid for it." She told one of her
boy toys who was so stoned all he
could manage was an obligatory,
"Bummer," his reaction to all negatives
like his all-purpose "Cool," for all
the positive things in life. Like
beer blasts and pill parties, unprotected
sex in beachfront houses while parents
were away at orgies of their own,
though they called them something else.

All the like-minded she witches in
her coven had matching tats on
their ass as a kind of blood kinship
thing that would forever unite them
in sisterhood until the next falling out,
next sex text one of them would send,

to one of their number, to like, everyone
on earth. Something sent as a kind of
joke, under the influence of alcohol
and E, barely remembered after, until
the message went, like viral, and the girl
in question thought razor blades
in the bath was the only solution
to an otherwise insoluble problem.
And it might have been, were it not
for the kid brother seeing the text,
and barging into that room no adult
would dare to go.
Accused of bullying, violating
sacred trusts, and child porn laws,
she stonewalls authorities, insists she is
above all this childish stuff and maybe
she was, in a way, if someone hadn't
almost died.

Andy Warhol Revisited

Made up with five shades
of mascara, all of them black,
she was a pan-angelic pixie
embarking on a second childhood
before a self-induced, early
death. Wants to be reborn,
fully formed, in the not-so-
distant past so she can screen
test for Warhol, be a fifteen
minute superstar, a major face,
as one of the Chelsea Girls,
the role she was meant to play.
Impossible to tell what her real
story was, though she will provide
a dozen prologues to one,
twice as many plot lines,
all of them variations on a tragic
theme that draws the listener closer
to inhale the musky scents of sex
and death that clung to her like
some kind of strange, alluring
body wash.
"What's the name of the perfume
you're wearing?" You ask.
"I call it Corpse Flower." She says,
but doesn't laugh.

You change the subject, wonder if
all her current needs are just as
bizarre: seduction, dominance,
betrayal, and pain, the more pain
the better the wounds and the scars
left behind to remember her by.

Out of Luck

I used to see him
all the time on
the bus wasted out
of his skull

He must have had
some kind of menial
job in Albany

The kind of employment
that kept him in beer
and rotgut

Work arranged for him by
the counselors of Conifer
Park

He'd last six weeks or so
a couple of months sometimes

Half a year on those
rare occasions when his bosses
understood a man's needs
for alcohol were stronger
that a man's ability to work

Though even the most
tolerant of bossmen needed
a warm body he couldn't provide
and he would get the axe

Faced the devil's dilemma:
30 days dry in rehab
or 30 days in County

I heard him tell some guy
it was the toughest decision
he ever had to make

Opted for rehab in the end
knowing future work depended
upon him having the cleanest
record possible

It's not like he was a hardened
criminal, "Shit, Man, I'm just
a drunk. Why don't people
let me be?"

By people I figured he meant
the not-so-little woman at home
and all those mouths he was
supposed to be feeding

So off he'd go and a month
or more later he'd be back
on the bus making some woman
wonder how this could be
happening to her

How her car could just die
the way it did leaving her
high and dry and shit out
of luck some stinking moron
trashed and falling asleep
against her shoulder
dead weight on the 55
all the seats taken and
nowhere else to go

White Girl on the Bus

If you weren't
looking to see
who was screaming
into her cell phone
on the bus

you'd swear the speaker
was a young black
woman

So exact were her
intonations
imitations of street
speech

The person to whom
she was speaking
surely the young black
man, father of her child

though she be denying
that she be just another honky
white chick fucking black
men for prestige

Told to watch her

language by the bus driver
she feels the need to
have the last word before
cutting everyone off

"I'm killing your baby"

Presses the off button
on her cell
pulls the bus rip cord
and alights by
Planned Parenthood

In five years, she'll be,
Maybe, twenty

Another perfect day for banana fishing

in this place of localized black holes
where the empties are thrown,
of garbage pits and firetraps,
the reek of kerosene and of rot,
skins of dead animals stretched out
like canvas sails on blood sample walls
as backdrops, blackout shades to keep
the light out, viscera still intact,
as flytraps insects are attached to as
if this place was the set for some ultimate
survivor reality show, the cannibal
episodes, featuring the Lord of the Flies
Live, outback, in some off the map place,
where the natives are inbred for genetic
impurities: mentally deficient, Ricketts
bent, social deviance in action as
pied pipers with PBRs and weed
instead of candy and ginger bread lures
into this forest primeval, Silence of
the Lambs sequel, bad endings assured
once the flaying knives have been unsheathed.

Scenes of a Summer Evening

Fog off dead calm sea in black
and white night, lone street light
flickers, fading in and out as if part of
some epileptic fit of a place,
of a Paris After Dark revisited,
where ghost people are in transition
between worlds, between two stations
of an underground railroad to nowhere,
a place where all transactions are phantom
ones: by the hour tricks for sickness prevention
fix, mesh stockings and mini-skirts,
dime bags and home lab Crystal,
a kind of spontaneous home movie,
where Satyricon dream shadows assume
a kind of living form, become as if newly born
and full grown, risen from somewhere way below,
searching for all the fuel they'll need to keep
an internal, eternal fire burning with a pure
but invisible flame.

Skinhead Fury

"amazing, the energy we burn fueling our anger"

His t-shirt said, Organized Anarchy,
white skulls rampant on a field of
burning crosses; skinhead fury
in crooked black lettering about to
ignite, race wars and random acts of
wanton violence his modus operandi
in between long stretches inside,
courtesy of the state judicial system.
Released, there was always hard core
Euro trash death metal, the American
Panzer division for entertainment,
tunes to rev by for out-of-control nights
on the town as a Jagermonster, chilled
shots on banzai booze with Red Bull
and Bourbon chasers, rocket fuel
for a mind whose brain has become
disconnected from his body, all the frayed
wires inside trying to relay, trying to
process all the incoming stimuli without
success, clicking onto automatic: hate
messaging and battle cries. The broken
thing standing, a wounded, feral animal,
bear baited for mayhem and bloodletting
sport; two stun guns and a baton can't
put him down.

Tastee-Freeze

Ensconced in sunny corner of
honky tonk bar off hours, spewing
inanities about his life, work and
imagined conquests, plans for
a non-existent future, he is
the flushed version of character from
some dead author's lost novel no one
in his right mind would ever read.
If he were the subject of
a painting, the work would
have a title like, "Nine Kinds
of Stupid" or "Study in Gray
Space Debris Jettisoned, Empty
Vessel Left Behind." Even the
preliminary sketches would be
a freak show grotesque in
the manner of Lucien Freud,
after Francis Bacon; a hung over
genetic anomaly, barely functioning
on Jolt Cola and Everclear,
a drink he referred to as a
Tastee-Freeze, something so lethal,
the imbiber's brain would experience
vapor lock, capillaries hardened,
blood flow restricted, disconnected
thoughts cascading from between
cracked teeth as bell shaped ice cubes.

Sober ten years, seven months, twenty-one days: a lament

The wife and I were holed up
in some place, not even sure
which wife, they all blend together
after a while. Might have been
the third one, that's when I was
at my worst, though it could just
as easily been the fourth one.
 I was bad then too.
All I know for sure was we had
all this cash on us, well, I had
all this cash, and it seemed like
totally necessary, vital even, to hide
some, bury it good, you know, just in case,
you know, for like one of those unknown
contingencies that inevitably turn up
when you're drunk. So we started
putting stuff in places: under mattresses,
cushion covers, under lamps, even in
the room safe and off we go to do
some damage, though, we called it
something else euphemistic, something
like a: night out on the town. There was
gambling where we were, either Vegas
or Atlantic City, you know how drunks
love to gamble and casinos love drunks.

Anyway, I'm sure I had some cards too.
once I shot my wad at craps and cards,
but they would have been in my wallet
which I shrewdly left back at the hotel,
whichever one we were staying at,
like no one forgets where they are staying,
right? This is back when hotels still
had room keys. We'd lost those a long
time ago along with the car keys.
Who knew what car we're driving?
I sure as hell didn't. I had lots of cars
back then. And money too. You think
stuff like that is going to last forever
when it's going good. Ha! So, I asked
the wife, "You know which car
we had?"
And she says, "The red one."
"They're all red.
"So."
"What am I supposed to, go out in
the parking lot and look for a red car?"
"Why not?"
Now you understand why I got divorced.
Anyway, we're in the lobby of
wherever, no room key, no car keys,
all my money in the room somewhere
and I'm tapped, so I ask the wife,
"Babe, you have any cash on you?"

"Gee, honey, I don't know.
You always say for me not to carry
cash because I spend too much when I do."
"Could you look, just in case.
We're going to have to crash some place
and we can figure out where the rest
of our stuff is later on. That's what room
service is for."
I'm leaning on the front desk counter
while she's rummaging through Pandora's
handbag, and I'm starting to freak
at all the stuff that's flying out of there.
I'm thinking, I'm going to need a fifth
of Jack Daniels to settle my nerves like, pronto,
when the night clerk taps me on the shoulder
and says, "Your room key, Sir."
It's almost enough to make you believe
in God. Actually, it was the drunk's precaution
of folding up a portrait of Andy Jackson
and slipping it to the kid on the way out
"to remember me by, in case I forget later on"
that saved the day. Still, I was so relieved,
I could have kissed the guy but I restrained
myself. For all I know, the wife is still
down in the lobby rummaging through
her bag. A sensible man would have
given up drinking right then and there
but no one ever accused me of having

a grain of sense. It would take something
a whole lot worse than losing a couple
of grand, a room key, a wife, and a car to
knock some sense into me.

A flat tire halfway to Vegas

Spare tire useless,
stranded somewhere between
hell, and nowhere, nearest cell
tower a Frankenpine in Southern
California, the only cars, ghost
vehicles rusting alongside the road
in midday sun, lost in some kind
of U-turn movie, somewhere a half
blind psycho mechanic the only
potential aid, along with a whole
sick crew of near-death locals,
driven mad by a lack of clean water
and the sun, surviving on locoweed
and cactus juice like the two outlaws
who appear, as if descended from the sky,
on some kind of magic carpet ride in
a rented, top-down convertible, red
Caddy, overinflated tires barely kissing
the concrete, and enough drugs in the trunk
to poison the water supply of three
Southwestern states, half as much again
inside their bodies, the first sign of life
in hours that could have been days,
stopping to offer a ride as they periodically
did for all the hallucinations, some more
real than others, and knowing there is no

choice, you accept the offer when the door
swings open and invites you inside,
"Hop on board young man and get ready for
the ride of a lifetime." A statement that is
no doubt true. And when they offer the contents
of what appears to be a box of Red Hots,
smiling the way the banditos do in "Treasure
of Sierra Madre" just before the ring leader
says, "Badges we don't need no stinkin' badges,"
you hesitate before accepting, but how can
you refuse?

Fucked by the muse

"I've seen things you people wouldn't believe"
      Roy Batty

In another life, she was a
gymnast, a nimble beauty,
supple as a loose limbed
acrobat, a synthesis of toned
body parts, weight training
and modern robotics, implants
that helped emulate muscle
memories of others, long past
their prime, or gone. Had a
whole set of new memories like
snapshots from a graveyard
transplanted from lost places into
active cells, retaining something
foreign as her own. At some
undefined point, her life became
uneven parallel bars, set slightly
askew. A few inches that could
have been miles, enough to upset
the balance, changing the glorious
to a ruin in the time, it takes two
wires to cross, spark and burn out
leaving only a scorched residue
behind. All the physical therapy

in the world could not restore
what was lost, all the whirlpool
baths meant to relax and heal,
becoming a swirling vortex pulling
her down to a place only Oxys,
Demerol and Jack Daniels could
cure. A few months of this kind
of intensive care, and she looked like
a crack whore made up for a Saturday
night in town looking for a trick
and a treat, feeling worse than
she looked.
"There's absolutely nothing I
wouldn't do for the right price.
Just name your amount and I'll consider it.
And that's no lie."
Had the competition medals and the rap
sheet to prove it.

Crazy

The war never ends on all
those twelve-hour shifts in
his mind, humping the night
as if it were a twenty-dollar whore
downloaded for action the duration
of a three-day pass.
Even stateside, mustered out,
nothing changed him, nothing altered
his focus, selling cash crops from
backdoor saloons, boatloads of pure
and suitcases of dinero, calling all
the shots for every deal that came
down, a posse of dead beat,
human moray eels on steroids
for protection, everywhere he went.
Downtime, clubbing with his crew,
was more of a black ops mission than
a special occasion. A date, grabbing
some babe and having her
strong armed into nearest empty
room for an up close and private
encounter, just her and the boys.
A wad of twenties and some blow
left behind, along with the wreckage
of her life. No one dared complain.
Not then. Not ever.

No one crossed him on a business
deal either since the rumor started
he might pop someone, anyone,
just for thrill. What he might do to an
actual offending party, unthinkable.
Out of town connections said he was
malo malo loco, was one tour of duty
and a deal from being lord of the
underground, a few heart beats
from immortal. No reason to change
the perceived, he thought. Not in this
life. Nor in any other.

The Little Darlings

They celebrated their thirteenth
birthdays under boardwalks,
felt sand in soft places rubbed raw
by young men who wore leathers
like emblems of doomed youth,
making love with pubescents,
another rite passed on their
journey to twenty-five to life
in some upstate pen they would
never leave.

The Little Darlings wore leopard skin
toreador pants that almost fit, matching
scoop top blouses and black bras when
they wore anything at all.

None of them had boyfriends
but all of them had fuck buddies,
interchangeable as spare parts,
some who worked better than others,
all of them with manufacturer's
defects.

Their single moms worked 9-5
that's PM to AM, turning tricks,
though they called it something

else, might see the sun six times
a year, by mistake, waking up
from some drug induced coma in
a place that let the outside in.
Brought home men who thought,
".45 long Colt, S&W, the gun
that you can't miss with" was gospel.
Had the words inscribed on their
chests in case someone needed
to quote chapter and verse.

No one cared what the Little Darlings
did when the adults weren't around
as long as the place didn't burn down
and they were quiet as choir girls, or, on
the nod, when they were.

The only book the Little Darlings
ever read was *Dancing on the Grave
of a Son of a Bitch*, found in a backpack
of some hippie chick they gang banged
for booty and for cash. Thought the title
sounded like the story of their lives
and, in a way, it was.

All the spare cash that wasn't spent
on weed, butts, or booze was stored
in a jar labeled, "Tips for Tats for Tits."

Their goal in life, to live until they
were sixteen; to acquire painted
birds and butterflies and affix them
to already-showing-signs-of hard-wear,
canvas of flesh.

Parallel Lives

Every city has one, a block God
forgot, some unofficial war zone,
demilitarized, but alive and active
with all the usual suspects cops roust
on periodic missions to clean up after
some particularly rowdy disturbance,
something so embarrassing, around
election day, even the mayor is moved
to act. After the votes have been counted,
results confirmed, the war goes on as before.
911 calls come in and cars are dispatched,
later rather than sooner, except, in cases
of extreme cruelty, events that make
front page news or, on occasion, CNN;
'Fraternity hazing involved terrorist
techniques, pledges for unchartered
frat subjected to punishments, not unlike
water boarding, until they were forced
to beg for mercy.'
The cries from basement/ dungeon so loud,
so horrific, even cowed neighbors
could no longer endure the noise, could
only imagine what must be happening inside.
University officials assert they had
'suspicions banned fraternity was still
accepting new members,' as they had been,

banding and disbanding time and time
again, for fifty years, only the names
and faces changed.
Over time, the block is modified,
buildings burned out, abandoned,
strafed in territorial feuds, boarded up
or razed, salt sprinkled on the mounds left
behind, for sale signs riddled with bullet
holes, gang graffiti ornamented, relics
no one cares to recall or revisit.
All the former denizens, drug dealers,
and their whores moved on, occupying
new digs that soon resemble the old:
from Odell to Kelton, from Elberon to
Quail to Washington; forsaken places,
reclamation projects so far past due
only those with no future go there.
Time Has Come Today

"You don't know what pain is."
Buffalo Bill

Somewhere along the line,
someone had put him in a metal cell,
a kind of prefab hurt locker,
and forgot to let him out. Maybe,
pounded on the sides to like, rattle
his cage every now and then,
never letting any unnecessary light in,
no food, no water, no human contact,
nada for days, so that when the family
business, literally, went up in smoke,
a mobile home, meth lab, defoliation
death trap, only he would survive
the fast-burning fireball suffused with
strange colors, sick smells of chemicals
and bad meat, a black hole where
the concrete pad had been.
He'd feel no remorse for confederate
flag ensemble wearing dad, a former
weightlifting skinhead gone to fat,
not completely weaned yet from his
Rebel Yell and his emaciated, toothless
straw haired, unwashed, skank of a woman,
something like thirty-nine going on
seventy, maybe his mother, maybe not.
Where he was going time was measured

in scorched spoonful's of street, ampoules
and syringes, black market product mined
from god's black earth.

Close Encounters of a Strange Kind

"You've got me hotter than Georgia asphalt."
Lula Pace

She made high heeled, mesh stockinged
love with the lead singers in bands
with names like: Thick Bastards,
Flaming Retards, Space Aliens for
Peace. Showed up for work bruised
and delirious, speaking the new language
no one could recognize, she'd learned
over the long weekend, wondering what
all the fuss over her was about,
"It's Wednesday. You were supposed
to be at work, as usual, on Monday."
"I guess I lost track of time."
"Don't bother coming back for your
last check. We'll mail it to you."
"Be that way."
And they were, eventually, at every
place she ever worked. When you looked
the way she did: sober, made-up, and faking it,
you got hired wherever you applied.
Were even cut some slack as if something
that gorgeous could never be as strung out as
she appeared. Might even be telling the truth
when she called in with a persistent stomach flu

that had sapped all her strength and left
her looking as if she'd spent the last
thirty-six hours sleeping in a snow bank
and had been thawed out by someone using
an acetylene torch. In fact, the closest she'd
been to snow was all those lines she'd been
snorting with the lead singer of Black Friday,
a half-dead, six foot eight, mixed race punk
rocker who called himself Raunch who
used his uncut-for-years dreds to hang dead
things from, "Like rodents and stuff. I think
we had sex. It was really weird."
If nothing else, these close encounters of
the strange kind made for entertaining texts.
Half the fun was figuring out who they were
from, what they expected of her and what
they might do next.

The European Tour

"She was the type of woman who would
have brought tears to the eyes of John Ruskin"
                    Maurice Dekobra

Her idea for a gap year was
to save all the tips she made
working as a cocktail waitress in
an upscale pub and from some soft
core hooking on the side. Soft core
hooking, to her, meant causal tricking
without a pimp, casual hints dropped,
beverage napkin dates, cell phone
numbers exchanged. "I like the older
guys. They have more money,
are more than likely married,
and don't ask questions and, man,
they expect the same. I don't do
perverted. Not for money anyway."
Was planning on doing the European
tour, on her back, first hand, in depth
research for a Baedeker's Guide
to Getting Laid, she was going to
call, *Do it on the Rails: Getting
the Most from Your Euro Pass
and Have Fun Doing It.* Something
like that, anyway. If that didn't work

out, her back up plan was a Sociological
study on the sexual habits of the horny
European Male: *You Don't Need
a Translator to Have Good Sex.*
Sociology wasn't her major, and she
couldn't write worth shit, but that
was something she'd worry about after
the research was finished, and recorded
in a diary she'd lose somewhere between
Buda and Pest. Thought protection during
intercourse was "for wimps, was like playing
Russian Roulette with an empty gun,"
when it was more like playing with one
chamber empty, high stakes stud poker
with someone else's money, drawing a card
for an inside straight.

Half Way to Hades

"'What would the prophet say if he
saw you in a place like this?'
'Pour me one.'"
Philip K. Dick

She promised him "a fucking
week of Christmas in hell,"
but could only manage a few days
of cooking voodoo chili so hot
their dreams were soaked with
sweat and blood, sheets torn into
strips for open wounds they nursed on
like succulents, passion fruits
from lands so distant they might
no longer exist. Nights, after hours
of rough sex, they licked the desert
heat from the short hairs on their
necks, sipping liquid fire from
the broken neck of Mescal Gusano
Azul, drinking Tecate from chests
half full of chips of dry ice, mist
rising from within to form circles
around the holes between clouds
where a full moon burned,
"I'll be your Maximilian, if you'll
be my Carlota." He said, in the collective

voices of all the no-longer-conscious
men they'd left behind along the road
they'd traveled of dancing dust devils
and death, "Shit, man, you take a girl
our for an ice cream sundae and end up
half way to Hades."
All the way, he thought, and then some.

Life Cycles

They are the worm people,
who sleep on funeral parlor castoffs,
barely worn sheets, a hundred hot rinses
could not remove the scent of death from,
an odor they wore like second skins,
peeling off as if once upon a time,
they'd spent too much time in the sun
and now all memory of it must be shed,
revealing an unnatural pallor of time spent
in airless caves, stagnant barroom holes,
inhaling each other's stale breath,
rust flaking from unwashed-for-decades
hair, no longer dandruff, but something
scaled, bed bug sores or skin ulcerations,
partially healed, leaking fetid fluids they
share like communicable diseases,
drinking the welfare checks of long-dead
relatives they claim as alive, forging
signatures, census forms, keeping the bodies
on ice in deep freezer chests until the power
fails and a new life cycle begins.

Misery

How pathetic am I?
I'll tell you.
I'd get so lonely,
so depressed reading
all those deadly lady poets,
you know the ones:
Sylvia, Sexton, that crew.
I'd be sitting on the couch
with one of Anne's books,
more than likely the fairy
tale one, or the awful rowing
thing, whatever, and I'd get
so blocked I couldn't even
write my own suicide note.
I'd decided to end it all
the way Anne did: in the garage,
with the car on and a shaker full
of bone-dry martinis; my own
little Doesn't Have a Clue game.
So don't I try it, and doesn't
the car run out of gas.
I pass out all right but don't I
wake up with a killer hangover,
one so bad that if I could have
dragged my sorry ass back inside
the house, I would have fallen on

a carving knife just to put myself
out of that misery.
No such luck.
What I get instead is this bunch of
misguided Angels of Mercy,
holding my hand and directing me toward
a righteous path to recovery.
Let me tell you, that scene is
a hell of a lot worse than dying
thoroughly liquored in the garage.

A Strange Comfort Afforded by Profession

Maybe I'd read too many books
when I was younger and they'd
gone to my head.
All that reading gave me a warped
point of view of the world, made
me unsuitable for what I did in
the world.
I mean, it's not normal for a bartender
to quote Chuang Tzu in order to explain
what I thought about, standing behind
the wood, watching the flames in
cocktail table candles burn down to
nothing.
My reply was always, "It's like the old man
said, 'If you stay in one place long
enough, everything that can happen, will.'"
They'd sort of nod, by way of reply,
and change the subject; after all I'd
been working in one place for over 20
years and I knew I was starting on
the second time around for everything.
What I should have said was, what I
meant, anyone who hung in a bar could
appreciate, something along
the lines of what Malcolm Lowry said
about being laid out flat on an outback

Mexico, cantina bar floor, drunk on Mescal,
something like, when the whole world
went careening by, totally out of control,
you need to try and grab something as it
whirls past.
Who could argue with that?

Just Be Yourself

My husband, Mr. Man of the World,
says, "Honey, I think I found the kind
of place you were thinking about.
It's dark and quiet and it looks like
it could be an Irish bar.
I'll bet you'll be able to get a nice Irish
coffee there."
I should have asked him what he was
betting but unfortunately, I didn't.
So, we go up to the door and this six foot
ten, 300 lb. guy is standing there with this
clipboard and all these limos are pulling up
and he says,
"What list you on, Sister?"
And I say, "Honey, I've got five kids.
I'm not on anyone's list."
"You're in." He says.
And I say, "I'm not sure if we really want to
go in."
"Sure, you do. Drinks are on me." The big guy says.
So, in we go.
We're looking around at all these roped off
sections and stuff, still not getting it,
I mean how were we supposed to know it was
like NCAA Week in NYC and this was like
the private club in Midtown Manhattan for all

the players? We're still puzzling stuff out
when this huge iron door opens and we're
almost blown off our feet by the bass.
We can't see much of anything at first
what with the spinning lights and all these tall
dark shadows on the dancefloor. I mean everyone
is six foot one hundred and those are the girls.
The guys are really tall. Some people might have
been fearful but not me. Anyone asks me what
we're doing here I could honestly say, 'We're Irish.
The door man said the drinks were on him.
Never let it be said the Irish would ever pass on
the promise of a free drink.' Hell, the whole of our
heritage depended upon what we were doing here.
We couldn't let our people down by not following
a solid promise for a free drink.
Let me tell you, we had a blast. They loved us.
And we loved them. It took a while to get used
to the Coors Light commercials being shown on
the bar ceiling, the spinning lights, plus that music
but we managed. Go with the flow, that's my motto.
That and, Just be yourself. Hell, I wasn't kidding
about that free drink business and everyone there
knew it too. Did their best to make sure we got
our due and more.

The Student Body

They called her the student
body though she didn't exactly
attend classes at the university
or anywhere else, though she did,
once, but she was bounced out
of where she was enrolled on
permanent social probation,
had been nabbed in the men's dorm,
when there were such things as
separate sex dorms, and it mattered
that they stayed that way.
She was caught giving head to some guy
in that age of man when a woman
could be locked up in a nuthouse
for giving a blow job and thereafter
be saddled with the nickname BJ no
matter what her given name was or who
her old man was.
I thought the ex-gyrene bartender who'd
told me her tale was like bagging me
but after I actually met her and we started
hanging out,
she was really cool about what
had come down. "Never mind what my
real name is, everyone is going to call me
BJ no matter what I say, so that's who I

am now. Everything they told you about
me is true. The worst of it will always be
that time I spent locked up with all those
freaks as if I were one of them. Every
campus, every college, every local hang out
has a Village Pump, the Fallen Woman,
the Hester Prynne Scarlet Letter woman
they can fuck, fuck over that is, and feel
superior to after it's all over; in this town
that would be me. It's a mistake to think you
can touch me, though." I thought,
maybe she was like bagging me as well, but
after a while I could tell she wasn't. That all
the stigmas and confinements and bullshit
had gone to her head and stayed there.

"Sometimes i just fall into it"
                                   Bukowski

Maybe it was the year, Winter of '69,
'70, four feet of frozen snow every-
where, Arctic winds blasting over open
fields, the lights from Utica State
beckoning across that vast, white
expanse. Maybe it was that useless
war I was eligible for, ready or not;
no prospects, nowhere to go, warm
flat beer in Styrofoam cup, two joints
of Mexican in my brain, a Sneaky
Pete pint in my back pocket, half-gone
and after that? After that, more staring
at the lights, sitting, as I was cross-legged
in far corner of game-room-by-day-
pub-by-night place, adamantly alone, depressed
and dreaming of how depressing it would
be not to be depressed, my friends blowing
me off, realizing it was useless to try and
rouse me from where I went without them,
not knowing I was seriously thinking of
never coming back and she said,
"I've never seen anyone as alone as you are."
And, I wondered who she might be and
why she might care, "I used to be that alone too.
And then I killed myself. In another life.

I'm back now for you." She said, holding out
her hand for me and I take it, allowing myself
to be guided into the night. As I go,
I can hear my friends laughing, loudly
talking among themselves, saying stuff
like, "Way to go." and "Strangest way I
ever saw to pick up a woman but if it works,
what the fuck." All those things they were
saying, as if I might be coming back.

I wish they'd stop

bringing up that cop killer business
as if that was all he ever did in his life

Man was my friend
Had to leave town for years
'cause those guys were always
dogging his ass

Comes back for a couple of days
to see some people, do a little
business and have a little fun
and what happens?

They crowd him and stuff happens
A man's got a right to defend himself,
don't he?

The Fireman

Funny seeing his face in
that paper after all these
years. I thought he was
one guy that was a long
shot for retirement. Last
time I saw him, he was
plastered long before noon.
I guess that's what you did
on duty in the fire house;
drink beer. There's a hell
of a lot of dead time when
nothing is shaking a few
beers helped a man to tide
over. Half of those hours
were day hours. Must
have cramped more than a
couple of guy's style when
the laws changed and beer
was taken off tap 24-7.
There was always someone
to designate as the driver,
to cover the action when stuff
came down when the shift boss
was totaled. I'm not sure how
they hushed up his
accident on the way home

from the bar. He was more
than a mess before he left
and it was his wedding
anniversary too.
Said in the paper he was still
married so they must have
covered that over somehow too.
His buddy the real estate guy
said it was all my fault. About
the accident. I let him think so
too. Wouldn't have done any
good telling him those G&T's
that Looie was drinking were
all T's with a small splash of G
on top for taste. He said I could
have taken his car keys. Not that
it would have mattered.
Guys like Looie always had a spare
set stashed somewhere just in case.
I'm glad Looie made it to thirty years.
In the long run, he made out a
hell of a lot better than the real
estate guy. His story didn't end
well. Life stories never do.

Old Man

at the bus stop
cadging cigarettes

right side useless
supported by a cane

stroke afflicted
mostly bald head

hidden beneath
old Yankees cap

nearly transparent skin

He looks oddly familiar
more familiar than he should

until I remember why,
remember how he used to brag

say how I'd made him
his first legal drink

when he was five years
younger than I was

before he became half dead
and twice my age

Skull Water

Half way into a week long
binge, the drink she settled on
was something called Skull Water:
Vodka Peppar, Everclear and
McGillicuddy's Peppermint Schnapps.
Said, "It tastes like something
salvaged from an excavated grave
remains pureed into a liquid form.
Yeah, it tastes like shit but it cures
what ails you." I looked her over
and saw a face ravaged by disease,
a Strawberry Fields Forever
t-shirt that she might have been
wearing when she died and was
resurrected from that grave she
mentioned early on. The rest of her
was a royal mess. I wondered
what she might have looked like
as a young woman. Something Goth,
for sure, or worse, a live model
for Suicide Blondes of America.

"So what thou wilt shall be the whole of the law"
A. Crowley

"Slick is what I am."
He thought. The slickest
thing on four wheels,
in a top-down, T-bird
convertible classic, an
ultra-charged super sport
on a Yugo budget, slick
as loose gravel on a soft
shoulder, a detour to an
Interstate that ended up
in a rathole neighborhood,
out of gas and closed-forever
inconvenience stores that he
would hide in the shadows
of, a widow maker in surplus
army fatigues. Even his
commando tactics were cheap
imitations of the real thing,
learned from watching Rambo
and his clones, you know,
the movies, rock groups,
solo artists with psycho ward
mentalities and a mean streak
as wide as blood puddles left
behind by two chicken playing

assholes too stupid not to refuse
to yield the right of way.
He figured he could get away
with just about anything: a heist,
a mugging, armed robbery, rape,
mayhem and murder. Even if
he somehow screwed up and got
caught, he thought he could
bullshit God; had the world
by the balls with vice grips
or so he thought.

Nominal Functional

The cast of his eyes suggest
some kind of demented mind,
not one of God's fools but
one tripping on a cocktail containing
warped amino acids, genes so bad
his basic wiring has a new kind of
alternating current, the kind that
is easily interrupted by any kind
of inclement weather, unfavorable
star charts, asteroid showers,
sun spots, bumps on the road
he coasts over in handicapped
seating, rocking back and forth
against the motion of the bus,
fighting the torque, all the immovable
forces in his life ganged up to deny
him easy access to anything,
even the speech, he uses as a weapon,
observing stuff no one else gets
to see, violently reacting to any
and all attempts to interrupt his
routine, especially at the home base
he maintains as a "nominal functional,"
living on his own with minimal
supervision, neither seeking nor
accepting constructive suggestions

such as, "You really need to think
about eating something else besides
Mars bars and drinking nothing but
Diet Coke," the two staples of his life
along with the Cartoon Network,
SpongeBob SquarePants and Road Runner
beeping in his brain, beeping his way off
a cliff, lighter than the air, defying
gravity, leaving him behind to fall
straight down, flailing, rocking against
reality, rocking, always rocking.

Name Brand Beers

My old man worked
for the Schaefer Brewery
and so did his dad.

You should see them;
bellies big as beer kegs,
two free cases a week
plus all you could drink
at work.

How could you beat a
deal like that? Free beer,
a pay check, and a pension too.

They got me on too.
I figured I'd work there
all my life just the way
they did. And when it was
my son's turn....

No one thought it would
ever end. Hell, no, it was
Schaeffer Beer, Man, a staple,
a standard but we all know
what it's about now, don't we?

The Almighty bottom line.

Don't know what I'm going
to do now, Man.

Well, they say bad things
always happen in threes,
guess that means us: three
generations of losers,
lives wasted, pissed
down a drain.

Pour me a Bud, I've got
some serious drinking to do.

Guardian Angel

His guardian angel must
have been packing some
serious heat, must have had
a small arsenal and enough
ammo to take out a small
army secured beneath her
flowing black robes.
She used a flaming sword
instead of head lamps to show
the way on dark, moonless nights
patrolling the deserts of his
life, a life that was soon-to-be
a ravaged wasteland
of stripped malls, gutted wild
animals hunted for their tusks,
their fur, then discarded and
left to rot beside lost pitted
highways that lead South
into the unknown.
He was so lost he followed
any jagged path that took
him away from where he was,
hoping for an end to all
the torments in this life
never imagining how nearby
the agent of his deliverance was,

what she would look like and what
the brutal nature of this wished-for
end would be.

"on and off the road"

After years of hearing people ask me
what else I did besides work behind the bar,
of asking me what my other job was as if
50 hours or so a week wasn't like real work,
as if ordering, stocking, inventorying and
selling close to a million dollars' worth of
booze in 1970's money wasn't work.
As if restaurant management was some kind of
slacker job for no minds and losers and drunks
like themselves. After all those seemingly
endless rounds of questioning, I developed
a stock response, "I'm independently wealthy
and I do this for fun." After a while I added,
"And I'm gathering material for a book."
Most people didn't want to know what kind of
book it was going to be. Maybe they thought
they would be in it and what I had to say wasn't
going to reflect well on them. And they'd be right.

When I grew older, changed jobs, been beat up,
threatened a few dozen times, and been fucked over
by professionals, I developed a real attitude to go
with my drinking problem. Now, I could honestly
answer any questions about my employment
situation by saying that I had reached a certain
stage in my life where I realized that I only had

two marketable skills. One was that I was a world
class ball buster and the other was I could make
drinks faster than seemed humanly possible.
Logically, I decided to combine the two talents
and here I am. I might have added that the hours
allowed plenty of time for serious drinking and
recovery and that it helped that being wasted was
a natural state in bar life and being that way yourself
allowed you to blend right in with everyone else
in ways that just weren't possible in most professions.

Still, persistent folks would insist, "But you're an
educated man. Why waste all those years in school?"
As if studying literature somehow prepared me for
life in the real world or provided ample opportunities
for employment. In fact, I often said, the most
useful course I ever took in college was Abnormal Psych
and I've seen nothing yet to change that opinion.
And I would continue, "Since when isn't bartending
educational? I've learned more in a half an hour
tending bar than I did
in seven years of full-time study at universities." I
didn't bother telling them that I was like a real live
professional poet too.
How were they ever going to understand that?

Townes Van Zandt, Waitin' Round to Die

in the rundown,
lowdown honky tonks
you played, barely alive,
your voice fed back:
pain, pain & more
pain, amplified by Bose
speakers, poem songs,
microphones drenched by
cheap beer, PBR's the one
you swilled the most so you'd
fit right in with all those
Rednecks and their women
who watched you play,
so you'd be so cool with
all the rest of the dead
beat losers on Nowhere &
Vine, so when the toll
collectors came around
for all those silver dollars
placed on your flat, dead
eyes instead of the copper
ones preferred by long dead
Greeks, you'd be primed
& ready to go. Once you get
this far down the road that
never ends, you have no

choice but to keep on moving
down the line, keep on moving
further along the lonely river
of Forgetfulness & of Death,
head bowed & empty, your voice
stolen by furies; hell, where you are
now, it doesn't matter which coin
of the realm you offered or
what words you might have written,
what songs you might have sung.

"All in a Night's Work"
after Cathy Porter

If I'd ever wondered where
old strippers went when they'd
passed their prime, I had an
answer sitting right next to me
at the bar chain smoking Lucky
Strikes and drinking Rye Pres's
one after the other, keeping
counsel only with herself,
never speaking, not even to order
another drink. When she was ready,
she'd just slide the empty high ball
glass across the wood, unwrinkled
another five-dollar bill and point
at the melting ice inside indicating
the new drink should go right on
top of the old one. Throwing her
ice away was a mistake new barkeeps
only made once. She had the vise
grip of a python that would leave
marks after it had been applied and
it wasn't something you wanted to
make a habit of encountering if you
could help it. Rumor had it, in her
prime, those dancer's legs could scissor
lock a man in one place past dawn,

though now, judging by the flesh
that showed on her face and arms,
the only death grip strength that remained
in her, was in that hand methodically
lifting the next drink and the last.

Flying with one wing

It was like some unofficial
class reunion in the tavern,
old home week, exchanging
news, "Whatever happened to
that, babe? Lauren, I think
her name was?"
"That was one righteous babe:
she relapsed. They violated
her ass big time. Took her kid
away. Put her in the joint.
She really loved that kid too."
"Too damn bad. I heard about
the Case Man."
"Yeah, he dumped that silly ass
bike of his just the way we said
he would. Damn fool was deep fried,
man. He one serious crispy critter now.
You hear about Tammy L?"
"I saw her on the News. She always
said she was gonna be a headliner.
And she was right."
"Yeah, but not the way she figured.
That girl had one titanic voice.
Always thought she shoulda gone
for American Idol. She coulda won
that easy if she coulda stayed even

slightly straight and sober."
"Ain't no residuals for gettin' your
face shot off."
"Not much future in it, that's for sure.
Anyone you know of go straight?"
"Hell, no. You don't go to no rehab
the first two, three times to get straight,
you go because, you're compelled to go."
"I hear you. Buy you another taste?"
"Hell, yeah. Can't fly on one wing."

Maybe it was meant

to be, to end this way,
a life spent on the edge
always playing a loser's
hand but pretending
otherwise, and fooling
no one, over his head
and drowning in a high
stakes poker game, gambling
away someone else's cash,
bluffing his way all
the way to a back room
in hell's half acre, every
thing riding on one, way
long shot, drawing to an
inside straight, a Royal
Flush in spades, baby,
missing only the dark
lady; the sad, long story
of his life, all rolled up
inside a layer of smoke
and bad overhead light,
trying to stare down a tag
team of professional plastic
surgeons sure he was
a sucker bet about to be
busted of a lone, down card

he's almost afraid to look
at, feeling its skin as if
somehow rubbing the out
side surface would grant
him the wish of a lifetime,
screwed five ways against
Sunday either way; nothing
left to do but slide the dealt
card in with the others, unfold
the new hand slowly, read
what they had to say and weep.

Child of the Great Depression

Her daughter was a product
of the Depression, not the one
before World War II but the one
that came after bouts of sustained
self-abuse, near-starvation after
drugs orgies and the other kind,
puking breakfast, lunch & dinner
but never dessert, the little snacks
she was handed under tables in
tightly wrapped foil packages,
sealed envelopes or found in
the pisser taped to the back side
of the tanks or inside, in sealed
plastic bags, a razor blade always
handy for cutting lines on compact
mirrors, the dust inside not rouge
but 3 to 7 years' worth of mandatory
time for first offenses, tastes of
bitter sweets she had to wash down
with Fleischman's 90 proof, no girlie
drinks with sipper sticks for her,
no fruit garnish that came stuck to
the sides of tulip shaped glasses, just
serious shooters, mainliners straight
to whatever vein was exposed
they were all for party purposes,

for sale at a price, everything and
anything, you name it, I'm game,
on this hellacious non-stop binge
that could last a lifetime and not
involve waking up afterwards,
not even on the locked-in ward
where she finally came to, lucky to
be alive and pregnant thinking
nothing could be worse than this
but what the hell did she know?

Doing the Right Thing

She was pregnant with his baby
and he was trying to make her
younger sisters in no particular
order, all six of them spaced
roughly a year apart, all party
girls ready and willing to be
wasted on whatever was available,
anything he would gladly provide
even though he was inevitably,
temporarily in between positions,
or just hired, sober for a week or
so, long enough to collect a check
or two, gradually reverting to old
habits, reducing the work load,
blowing off shifts, not showing at
all, and when he did, wasted beyond
belief and useless, half pints of gin
always on-hand to mix with 7 Up,
Teem, Ginger Ale in a pinch, the kind
of a gentleman who would offer
to marry the one he knocked up,
figuring she would tell him to get
lost given how obvious he was
around the sisters, though, to his credit,
he followed through with the marriage
though it was all too painful, all too clear

that it was too late for all of them,
even the baby.

Refugee from Another Planet

Whatever Way Out Machine
he'd come in on must have
malfunctioned and left him
stranded still dressed in
decades-before-the-millennium
duds: bright floral surfer pants,
loud striped t-shirt, leather thongs
and rose-colored glasses that
mostly concealed his drug spaced
eyes. He was trying to hitch
a ride to the coast to join
an enclave of pot growers
and potential cult suicides,
the name of his destination
tattooed on his forearm in code,
a place eight miles past nowhere
at the bottom of a cliff that
a Richter Scale 8 had dumped
into the Pacific, not even memories
left behind.

Snow Crash

Riding the stainless steel
slope to nowhere, fighting
the blizzard, his eyes are
as hard as freeze-dried spit
glazed by a gale force wind,
was the way his life was a
few drinks short of death.
Walked with one ski pole
broken off at the point,
the other implanted in ice
as a slight handicap
to make life more interesting
on those night you could hear
him calling out from a mile
away as he made his way
toward the bar, the inside
of his head a perfect tequila
azul, his wet brain soaking in
a lemon-lime emulsion,
the salt lick of his lips
white as death.

Kamikaze Pilots

"You tend bar the way
kamikaze pilots fly missions."
The old guy said.
"How's that?"
"Complete disregard for yourself,
anyone, anything in your way;
it's just the mission that counts."
I wasn't sure if that was
a compliment or not.
I figured it wasn't.
I was more used to people
throwing things at me than
praising me. I was a known
spoil sport; always tossing
monkey wrenches into people's
dysfunctional plans for the evening,
which usually involved some sort of
malicious mischief and mayhem.
Sometimes pillaging and raping
if they were lucky, and the action
got really hot. I had to admit,
the old guy's observation had some
merit, as I did tend to intently focus
on the business at hand, blocking out
anything that got in my way of
completing a transaction, multi-
tasking up the ass; the busier it got
the more intent I became, the more

balls I kept balanced in the air.
Sometimes it got so crazy, working
could almost be fun, doing the near
impossible routinely; fun that is,
if your heart didn't give out or
some asshole didn't try to get one
over on you. There are always assholes
and you only had one heart that wouldn't
stay young forever.
"If I were you," The old guy was saying,
"I'd tear a muscle real bad or "fall"
down the stairs on the way to changing
a keg. A guy could get a permanent
injury that way and collect for life
if he worked the system right."
"Not my style."
"I figured that. You really are as crazy
as you look. A real Johnny B. Goode."
"That would be me in spades."
The old guy was an ex-union man,
not me. I was above all that. Though,
as I got older, the missions got harder,
the balls in the air, heavier and harder
to juggle, and I started feeling like that
pilot the old man referenced: heading
down fast, not worried about what got
in my way or how hard I was about to hit.

Cheating Death

What can you say about a guy
who answers to the name of
Asshole? Except he's the kind of
guy you'd throw a party for the day
after being drafted in the down and
dirty years of Vietnam. He wouldn't
be the first guy you'd throw a going
away party for, nor the last, but he
was the only one who came back.
Had his draft notice rescinded pending
the lottery and drew a number so
high they'd take women and children
before they took him. Returned to drink
all your booze, raid the fridge, not
do dishes or clean, stay up all night
watching old movies, the test patterns,
the white noise in his head static
electricity that kept his body breathing
while he slept all day, rising only
to do a few numbers, down some of
his personal stash and drive someone
else's car, using all their gas and
accumulating tickets he would never pay.
He was everyone's worst nightmare,
the roommate from hell, especially when
there was a woman around he could spy on

behind closed doors, not even bothering to
suppress his animal instincts, heavy breathing;
thought invading privacy came with
the territory of occasionally paying rent.
It just seemed so grossly unfair
someone like him, that asshole, could
cheat death. Something he thought
so funny he'd get in your face, telling
everyone to send him a picture from
Basic without hair, and how you'd look
good in green, and how he'd be sure to be
drinking a beer while you were having your
balls shot off in some jungle on the other side
of the world. It was a miracle he survived
what he was saying with only one fat lip
and a black eye. Still, he couldn't survive
driving drunk, a black ice S curve, a steep
drop into a barely frozen lake. Everyone
knew whose car it was in there and who was
inside, wouldn't have bothered fishing him out,
or, to look inside, just to make sure, but they had to.
It was the law.

Vietnam

His T-shirt said, red letters
on a field of black. Cutoff
sleeves, jagged tear in fabric
just above the heart suggests his
body may have returned from a
place of engagement but his mind
was still there with the carpet
bombs, Agent Orange, Dioxin
death raiders, daisy cut to the bone;
chin stubble still growing though
his head had long ago been removed.

Wandering in the cage

Captured high riding red Honda bikes
at Charlie/ Khmer checkpoint assuming
they'd be released, detained for brief
interviews, interrogations; arrogant or
naïve, or just plain crazy no one knows.
They expected to return with the story
of a lifetime, tales to be told and embellished
over endless pipes of the local weed, heavy
hit, as non-combatants front loaded with
cameras, more balls than brains, composing
shots for wire service release, cover articles
at Life, Time, Paris Match, finding instead,
Year of the Monkey misfortune during
escalating hostilities, bomb-them-back-
to-the-Stone Ages mentalities, no release
imminent, possibly friendly fire wounded,
jungle fevered, confined to bamboo cages
to be pissed on, tormented, prodded, and poked,
regularly beaten as white demons, photo
journaling hell from inside the Inferno.

Smoking Opium in Danang

Wilfred Owen wrote of strange,
hypnotic beauty of flares, at night,
firing over no man's land, where
he was soon to be dead himself
a couple of weeks before Armistice.
In Vietnam it was the pipes of many
dreams that brought visions,
fears of being overrun, sappers
sneaking beneath concertina wire
and reversing mines, of all the mad
minutes that lasted forever inside
and out of free fire zones.
Or they were Air America spooks on
no story, what missions, by the edge
of the jungle, on a nowhere perimeter,
they are lurps, long range reconnaissance
patrol men, highly trained ghost soldiers,
smoking pure dope and watching what
moved in the endless nights of their dreams.

Ashes and grief

Where I'm living these days is
like a second tour of duty in the Nam,
doing a house to house, clearing
the streets, search and destroy,
every place you go, every day you do it,
winning their hearts and minds.
Lots of those boys, then, was lame honky
motherfuckers but they had my ass
and I, sure as shit, had theirs.
Got so tight over there we breathed
the same air, bled the same blood
and anyone who says any different don't
know squat. Last time I felt anything
remotely like pain was seeing one of those
suckers get dusted catching a mortar
round, waist high and moving fast.
Shit, when the smoke cleared there
was nothing left but a pair of boots
full of blood, two leg stumps still inside.
Like the man said when it's over, "it's
all ash and grief." Only difference now,
The Man catches your ass, he gonna
lock your ass up. Man coming after me
better had been good and dedicated cause
I'm playing hard to get and planning on
staying that way.

"how grimly we hold onto our misery"
Bukowksi

Whored out and drug sick,
bumming cigarettes from half-
dead sailors in cheap side
taverns, one foot in the grave
and the other about to slide,
sharing tokes with lung sick
losers, needles with a dying
breed, eyes, and mouths like
a mad dog's in the morning,
a dead one at night, still standing
but about to fall, prayer flags
from lost tribes affixed to wrists,
body prepped for plain air burial
on baked tar barroom roof, junkyard
rats in shadows, watching.

Forgotten Heroes
After Tom Taylor

The dead man's clock has no
hands for charting the backward
progression of time into cluttered
rooms, relics of a life broken into
ossuary rooms, each containing
forbidding objects of misspent
passion and solipsistic deeds,
the disharmonic sounds of old soldiering
homes and the crippling diseases
that placed them there, dependent
on brain killing drugs, neuroleptics
that induce visions no dream quest
can erase, though the image clusters
remain, surrounding them with objects
as an inducement to fear. Leaning back
in their uneasy reclining chairs, they must
endure nightly bombing raids, missions
they fly in their minds more real than
the ones they actually partook in, sounds
of the bombs landing outside, inducing them
to flee, to seek shelter from fire storms
and holocaustic ruins, unable to motivate,
wired as they are, to IVs wrapped around
government issued weapons instead of poles,
heart monitoring machines unplugged

along with ventilators, monitors, for continued sustenance and life. Only the human skull resting on top of the portable TV with lit cigarettes in each eye hole, seems capable of creating a new existence beyond this one.

Still Life with Policemen

A scatter of broken bottles,
colored glass, jagged necks
and curved edges, random splatters
on scuffed concrete, sidewalk
curb, and gutter where fluid
puddles, water, blood and
something else, maybe spilled
gasoline, maybe not. Red painted
fire hydrant draped in yellow scene
tape, looped through parked
car door handles, over wooden
saw horses: late afternoon shadows,
three men in uniform, another in
a suit staring down, hands in pockets
or pointing out details others may
not have seen. Squad car radios,
dispatcher's voice, slowed traffic
noises so far offstage they cannot
even be assumed.

"There will be no rest even in our dreams"

of Argentina, Chile, Ciudad Juarez,
Narcos in death cars, super charged
Falcons, running product for drug
warlords, cartels, collecting students,
intelligentsia, factory working girls for
midnight rides to desert outposts, pampas
out backs, torture chamber prisons to be
raped, beaten, electrocuted, to become
among the missing, *desaparecidos,* dead,
dropped from helicopters or held up for
fusilados, shot by informal firing squads,
goons who ride only at night when the moon
is down, faces blackened by coal dust or
hidden behind balaclavas, lights out on
their no license plate cars when they come
into towns no one sleeps in after dark.

Karaoke Killers

In Malaysia, in the Philippines,
in Thailand, eight killed, wasted
for singing John Denver's,
"Take Me Home Country Roads"
though the article doesn't say
whether it was the rendition, or,
the actual choice of song, that got
them killed. In some states singing
along with John Denver, even in
the privacy of your home, is a
capital offense. In Seattle singing
Cold Play off key can get your face
rearranged in a bar by a woman.
In the Philippines singing "My Way"
is a risky undertaking; six dead
and counting, ten years of serial,
unsolved murders, all related to
an Old Blue Eyes tune. Just think of
all the clubs and bars in this country
alone that song is sung in and what that
could mean; mass murderers with
Sinatra t-shirts, "Keep the song book pure."
Good thing the Sex Pistols are already
dead. I wonder, do the karaoke killers
hang loose in clubs waiting for certain
types of victims, do they profile, do

they take requests? "Walk on the Wild
Side," "Eve of Destruction,"
"Ballad of the Green Berets,"
"Black Leather Jackets and Motorcycle Boots."

"Nary a potential suicide in sight"

"We all pay. One way or the other."
    James Lee Burke

They looked as if they'd spent most
of their lives on the fringes of pool
parties sponging off people who
actually earned money doing something
even if it was some morally challenged,
high power job screwing people to walls
as if they were apprentice grand inquisitors
in designer shirts attracting human moray eels
wearing bad lounge wear bought with
dwindling trust fund cash not spent on
necessities like crank and blow.
These hangers on whose social skills extend
as far as talking to the ubiquitous zombie girls,
kept women, subsisting on chilled Polish vodka
and Black Beauties bitching about how life sucks
and which one of their girlfriends OD'd in
the guest house shitter and how they brought her back.
No one actually dies in their world, though
lots would like to. The ones that beat the odds
and become hand maidens to the Grim Reaper
are relegated to isolated corners of whatever
parties they buy it at, strategically placed out
of the way with a drink in one hand and an unlit

cigarette in the other, sunglasses shielding
their eyes from harsh lights of night and day
just like always, until everyone moves on to
the next happening soiree and the staff assumes
control; everything that remains disposed of as trash.

Songs of Love and Hate

"you listen to a dead man's music"
She said:

Songs of Love and Hate, on auto-
replay, "It's four in the morning
the end of December...."
over and over until Cole Porter's,
"Will it be cyanide or champagne?"
no longer seems to be a choice but
a matter of acquiring and mixing
the two.

Head so heavy with remorse and
alcohol, Valium, and white wine,
changing the notional voices inside as
difficult as altering the auto-play
selection. Freezing rain coats my soul
inches deep, all that black ice and not
a chipper in sight.

Scanning the mixed tapes on the shelves:
"Single Fantasy": John Lennon sings solo,
Branch Davidian David Koresh Memorial
Album: "Light My Fire" The Doors,
"Fire" Crazy World of Arthur Brown,
"Ring of Fire" Johnny Cash

"Love Hurts" Roy Orbison....
"Plane Crash Wilbury's": Buddy Holly,
The Big Bopper, Richie Valens,
Patsy Cline, Otis Redding, Ricky Nelson
singing "That's All She Wrote" ....

Songs of Love and Hate.

The Patience of the Deranged

All night she sits staring
out over the harbor
out into the night at what moves
and what does not

All night she bounces a hard
rubber ball on our wooden table

Catches it and drops it again
only pausing in her rhythmic acts
to light her unfiltered cigarettes
she smokes one after the other
while I try to sleep
in the small four posted bed
in the far corner of the undivided room

While I lie behind the mosquito
net curtains all night every night
for weeks thinking: she never sleeps

Nor do I

Acknowledgements

Art Mag: Another perfect day for banana fishing

Skinhead Fury

Tastee-Freeze

A flat tire halfway to Vegas

Asylum Floor: Sober ten years

The European Tour

Beatnik Cowboy: Ashes and Grief

Big Hammer: Patience of the Deranged

Chiron Review: On and off the road

Clark Street: Fucked by the Muse

Creativity Webzine: European Tour

Dumpster Fire Press: Refugee from Another Planet

5 AM: Still Life with Policemen

Great American Poetry Show: Forgotten Heroes

Heeltap: Cheating Death

Horror Sleaze Trash: Dancing Girls of Death

Citizens for Decent Literature: Andy Warhol Revisited

Mas Tequila: Karaoke Killers

Never Cowboy: Old Man

Penny-ante-feud: Scenes from a Summer Evening

Poet Plant Press Anthology: The Introduction

Red Fez: The Little Darlings

Rusty Truck: Crazy

Close Encounters of the Strange Kind

Schuylkill Valley Journal of Arts: Child of the Great Depression

Skidrow Penthouse: Found Photo: Alexandra like a Wraith
UFO Gigolo: Life Cycles
Underground Verse: "alone and insane in tiny rooms"
Up the River: Living the Dream

About the Author

Alan Catlin worked for the better part of 34 years in his unchosen profession as a barman in and around the greater Albany, NY area. He has published dozens of chapbooks and full-length books focusing on his work and the people he met while laboring in the trenches of bar warfare.

MORE ROADSIDE PRESS TITLES:

By Plane, Train or Coincidence
Michele McDannold

Prying
Jack Micheline, Charles Bukowski and Catfish McDaris

Wolf Whistles Behind the Dumpster
Dan Provost

Busking Blues: Recollections of a Chicago Street Musician and Squatter
Westley Heine

Unknowable Things
Kerry Trautman

How to Play House
Heather Dorn

Kiss the Heathens
Ryan Quinn Flanagan

St. James Infirmary
Steven Meloan

Street Corner Spirits
Westley Heine

A Room Above a Convenience Store
William Taylor Jr.

Resurrection Song
George Wallace

Nothing and Too Much to Talk About
Nancy Patrice Davenport

Bar Guide for the Seriously Deranged
Alan Catlin

MORE ROADSIDE PRESS TITLES:

Born on Good Friday
Nathan Graziano

Under Normal Conditions
Karl Koweski

The Dead and the Desperate
Dan Denton

Clown Gravy
Misti Rainwater-Lites

Walking Away
Michael D. Grover

All in a Pretty Little Row
Dan Provost

These Are the People in Your Neighbourhood
Jordan Trethewey

They Said I Wasn't College Material
Scot Young

Radio Water
Francine Witte

And Blackberries Grew Wild
Susan Mickelberry

Licorice Heart
Miles Budimir

Disposable Darlings
Todd Cirillo

Full Moon Midnight
Belinda Subraman

MORE ROADSIDE PRESS TITLES:

Innocent Postcards
John Pietaro

Cistern Latitudes
James Duncan